The Story of Our Holidays

JUNETEENTH

Joanna Ponto and Angela Leeper

Enslow Publishing
101 W. 23rd Street
Suite 240
New York, NY 10011
USA

enslow.com

To my husband, Brad, for all of his love and support

—Angela Leeper

Published in 2017 by Enslow Publishing, LLC.
101 W. 23rd Street, Suite 240, New York, NY 10011

Library of Congress Cataloging-in-Publication Data

Names: Ponto, Joanna, author. | Leeper, Angela, author.
Title: Juneteenth / Joanna Ponto and Angela Leeper.
Description: New York, NY : Enslow Publishing, 2017. | Series: The story of our holidays | Includes bibliographical references and index. | Audience: Age 8-up. | Audience: Grade 4 to 6.
Identifiers: LCCN 2016021419| ISBN 9780766083387 (library bound) | ISBN 9780766083363 (pbk.) | ISBN 9780766083370 (6-pack)
Subjects: LCSH: Juneteenth—Juvenile literature. |Slaves—Emancipation—Anniversaries, etc.—Texas—Juvenile literature. | African Americans—Anniversaries, etc.—Juvenile literature. | Slaves—Emancipation—Anniversaries, etc.—United States—Juvenile literature.
Classification: LCC E185.93.T4 P66 2017 | DDC 394.263—dc23
LC record available at https://lccn.loc.gov/2016021419

Printed in China

Portions of this book originally appeared in the book *Juneteenth: A Day to Celebrate Freedom from Slavery.*

Contents

Chapter 1

Free at Last!. 5

Chapter 2

The Road to Juneteenth. 8

Chapter 3

The First Juneteenth Celebrations 15

Chapter 4

Making Juneteenth a Holiday. 20

Chapter 5

What Is Juneteenth Like Today?. 23

Cooking on Juneteenth. 27

Juneteenth Craft 28

Glossary 30

Learn More 31

Index. 32

Children and adults march in the Juneteeth parade in Harlem, New York.

Free at Last!

It is a sunny day in Texas. A parade marches by. Cowboys and cowgirls ride horses down the street. Marching bands play music, and floats with many colors drive by. An African American family claps as they watch.

After the parade ends, the family goes home. More family members come over. They have a barbecue in the backyard. Ribs cook over a fire. Everyone drinks red soda pop.

Some family members play baseball. Others tell stories from the past. At night, fireworks light the sky. Everyone thinks about freedom.

This is not the Fourth of July (Independence Day). This is a special holiday for African Americans. On this day, they celebrate their freedom from slavery.

Life as a Slave

When the United States was new, many African Americans were slaves. They belonged to white slave owners. Slaves were property, like land or a house. They could be separated from their families at any time.

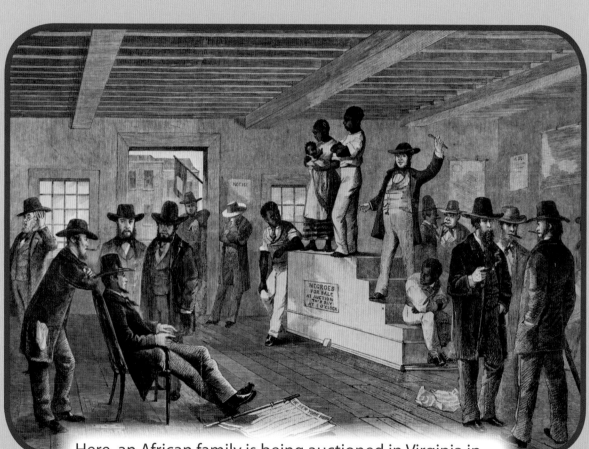

Here, an African family is being auctioned in Virginia in 1861. Often families would not be kept together. They had to go with whomever purchased them.

Slaves had a hard life. They worked long hours without pay. They could not go to school. Slave owners could sell their slaves or beat them whenever they wanted to. Some slave owners were very cruel.

Finally Free

In Texas, all slaves found out they were free on June 19, 1865. This day is known as Juneteenth. At first, it was a holiday in Texas. Today, people celebrate Juneteenth all across the United States.

On Juneteenth, African Americans remember their ancestors. Ancestors are the people who lived before us. On this day, many African Americans also think about the future. They want all African Americans to have a good life. African Americans think about their own lives, too. They think of ways to be good people.

We all need to remember Juneteenth. A sad time in history ended on this day. But every June 19, all Americans can celebrate freedom.

Chapter 2

The Road to Juneteenth

In order to understand the importance of Juneteenth, it is important to know something about African American history. The first Africans arrived in America at Jamestown, Virginia, in 1619. At this time, Virginia was a colony that belonged to England. It had many farms and plantations. These first African men and women worked on the farms and plantations as indentured servants to pay for their passage to America. But as time went on, Africans were brought to America to work as slaves.

Slavery and Southern Plantations

As more colonies were formed, plantation owners needed more slaves for labor. Millions of African slaves were brought to

COTTON-FIELD.

Enslaved Africans spent hours working in the hot sun on southern plantations. They planted and harvested crops, such as cotton, among other jobs.

America between the 1680s and 1865. Many worked on plantations that raised tobacco, rice, and cotton.

The colonies wanted to become their own country. On July 4, 1776, the colonists declared their freedom and fought against Great Britain in the Revolutionary War. The colonies won their freedom and became known as the United States of America.

Freedom for Some

Today, the United States celebrates this freedom, or independence, on July 4, which is called Independence Day. But not all Americans became free on July 4, 1776. African Americans remained slaves.

After the Revolutionary War ended, most slave owners lived in the southern part of the United States. Many people in the North were against slavery. The North and South could not agree on many issues. One of the biggest issues was slavery.

A Nation Divided

As a result, eleven states in the South seceded, or left, the United States in 1860 and 1861. The Confederate states breaking away from the Union began the American Civil War.

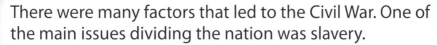
There were many factors that led to the Civil War. One of the main issues dividing the nation was slavery.

Abraham Lincoln was president during the Civil War. He did not believe that people should be slaves. On January 1, 1863, he issued the Emancipation Proclamation, a document that granted slaves in every state their freedom. Because the country was at war, the South did not obey this proclamation.

The Civil War ended on April 9, 1865, when the South surrendered to the North. All slaves in the Confederate states were finally supposed to be free. Because there were no telephones, televisions, or Internet, the news of emancipation spread slowly. Some people did not find out about the end of the war until weeks or months later.

Some slave owners did not tell their slaves about the end of the war. These African Americans did not know that they had been freed. The army was sent into the South to make sure that African American people understood their new freedom.

Texas was the farthest state that had seceded from the Union. African Americans there were some of the last people to hear about the Emancipation Proclamation and the end of the Civil War.

Freedom for All

On June 19, 1865, Major General Gordon Granger read a document called General Order Number 3 to the citizens of Galveston, Texas. This order explained that according to the Emancipation Proclamation, slaves in Texas were free. This was about two and a half months after the end of the Civil War. It was almost two and a half years after the Emancipation Proclamation had been issued.

The Constitution is the chief set of laws of the United States. Amendments, or changes, have been added to the Constitution to

The Emancipation Proclamation allowed black soldiers to fight in the Union army. Around two hundred thousand black soldiers fought to end the war and slavery.

update the laws. The Thirteenth Amendment to the Constitution was ratified, or approved, in 1865. This amendment officially ended all slavery in the United States.

Today, African Americans remember the end of slavery with the Juneteenth holiday. It is celebrated every June 19, the same day African Americans heard about their freedom in Galveston, Texas, in 1865.

Chapter 3

The First Juneteenth Celebrations

On June 19, 1866, one year after Major General Granger read General Order Number 3, the African Americans in Texas proudly celebrated the first Juneteenth holiday. They continued the tradition each year thereafter. These early celebrations often began with parades with floats and marching bands playing music.

Former slaves marched proudly in their towns. During slavery, there were even laws against African Americans dressing up. They could not walk the streets freely either. Now,

This engraving shows African Americans celebrating after hearing they are free.

African Americans were free to dress up in new clothes and march in the streets as they wished.

Serious Matters

Juneteenth was a serious time. The Emancipation Proclamation and General Order Number 3 were read. Former slaves told stories about their lives and how they fought against slavery. Religious leaders, educators, and former slaves gave moving speeches. They encouraged African American people to live and work honestly. African Americans went to church services to give thanks to God for their new freedom.

A Time for Fun, Too

Juneteenth was also a time for fun. Family members gathered for picnics and family reunions. Lamb, pork, and beef were cooked in barbecue pits. These were special meats. Not everyone could afford these foods every day. Other special foods included red soda pop and homemade cake and ice cream.

There were many ways to celebrate. Some African Americans listened to music and attended dances. Others went fishing. The

Harriet Tubman is a celebrated African American and former slave. She is famous for her role in the Underground Railroad, which helped enslaved African Americans escape north.

most popular activities were playing baseball and watching cowboys in rodeos.

All these traditions started in Texas. Some African Americans left Texas and moved to other states, such as Oklahoma, Arkansas, Louisiana, California, and Florida. They took these traditions with them and celebrated Juneteenth in their new locations.

Chapter 4

Making Juneteenth a Holiday

Juneteenth is the oldest African American holiday. Representative Al Edwards from Houston, Texas, wanted to make Juneteenth a legal state holiday in Texas. On holidays that are officially recognized by the government, people do not have to go to work. Government offices, schools, banks, and post offices are closed. This lets people spend more time with their families to celebrate.

Representative Edwards introduced a bill in the Texas legislature, where state laws are decided. The bill would make Juneteenth a legal state holiday. It was passed on June 7, 1979, and became a law. Juneteenth was celebrated as a legal state holiday for the first time on June 19, 1980.

Other states now honor Juneteenth as a holiday. These states include Delaware, Oklahoma, Georgia, Florida, Idaho, Iowa, Vermont, Alaska, Washington, Maryland, Kentucky, and Louisiana. In some states, Juneteenth is a legal holiday. In other states, it is an

On Juneteenth, people celebrate African American accomplishments and people who have shaped American history, such as Barack Obama, the first black president.

observed holiday, like Flag Day, Mother's Day, and Father's Day. Many other states have introduced bills that would make Juneteenth a state holiday. Some organizations are trying to make Juneteenth a national holiday so that all Americans can honor the day. In 1997, the United States Congress proclaimed June 19 "Juneteenth Independence Day."

Many Juneteenth celebrations take place across the United States. Some of the biggest celebrations are held in Milwaukee, Wisconsin; Minneapolis, Minnesota; Chicago, Illinois; Berkeley, California; Atlanta, Georgia; and Richmond, Virginia. Other major cities hold Juneteenth celebrations, too. Yet the biggest celebrations of all are still in Texas, in the cities of Houston, Dallas, Austin, Fort Worth, and San Antonio.

Chapter 5

What Is Juneteenth Like Today?

African American families still get together for Juneteenth just as they did in the 1800s. They watch parades like their ancestors did. Bands are still a part of the parades. Cowboys ride on their horses. African American members of community groups and the military march, ride horses, or ride on floats. Floats are now pulled by cars instead of horses. One float may carry Miss Juneteenth. Today, there may be Juneteenth activities throughout the entire month of June.

The Emancipation Proclamation and General Order Number 3 are still read out loud today. Religious leaders, community

Miss Juneteenth waves to the crowds during Denver's Juneteenth parade.

leaders, and educators still give speeches and tell stories about the fight to end slavery. They talk about abolitionists like Harriet Tubman and Frederick Douglass. These people believed that slavery was wrong. They helped to end slavery.

They also talk about civil rights leaders, such as Reverend Dr. Martin Luther King Jr. and Rosa Parks. These leaders helped African American people in the 1950s and 1960s. They wanted African Americans to have the same rights as white people. Some of these rights included going to schools with white students and voting. Both abolitionists and civil rights leaders risked their lives to help African Americans. On Juneteenth, many of these brave African American people are remembered.

Many other Juneteenth traditions continue today. African Americans still go to religious services and picnics. They tell family stories. They participate in baseball games, foot races, rodeos, and dances. Red soda pop, barbecue, and other foods from early Juneteenth celebrations are still popular today. Some African Americans celebrate with new clothes. Fireworks now end the long day.

New Traditions

Music has also become a large part of Juneteenth. There are many gospel and jazz concerts on or around Juneteenth.

Today, there is even a national celebration in the nation's capital, Washington, DC. It is called Washington Juneteenth. This Juneteenth celebration

Juneteenth is a good day to remember people like Martin Luther King Jr. King worked hard to gain equal rights for African Americans.

Communities around the country celebrate Juneteenth each year. This community barbecue is taking place in Roxbury, Massachusetts.

is like many others around the country. It includes religious services, speeches, and music concerts.

Juneteenth remains an important holiday for African Americans. It is still a time for thinking. African Americans continue to remember the horrible time of slavery and the brave men and women who fought to end it. Juneteenth also still means looking to the future. African Americans continue to help each other become better people.

Juneteenth is a time all Americans need to remember. We can all celebrate the end of slavery. We can respect each other and be glad that all Americans are free today!

Cooking on Juneteenth
Corn Muffins

Ingredients:

1 cup cornmeal
1 cup all-purpose flour
1/3 cup sugar

2 tbs baking powder
1 tsp salt
1 egg, beaten
1 cup milk
¼ cup canola or vegetable oil

Cornbread was a cheap and easy food for former slaves to make. It is still a popular dish in the South. Try this tasty corn muffin recipe for Juneteenth.

Directions:

1.) Preheat oven to 400°F. Using a spray oil, grease a muffin pan or line with paper muffin liners.

2.) In a large bowl, combine cornmeal, flour, sugar, baking powder, and salt. Stir together until fully mixed.

3.) In a medium bowl, combine egg, milk, and oil.

4.) Slowly pour the wet ingredients into the dry ones, a little at a time, stirring between each addition.

5.) Spoon the batter into prepared muffin cups.

6.) Bake for 15–20 minutes or until the muffins are golden brown and an inserted toothpick comes out clean.

* Adult supervision required.

Juneteenth Craft

Decorate for Juneteenth. Make some pinwheels to place in your garden, yard, or window!

Here are the supplies you will need:

construction paper
scissors
markers or crayons
push-pin or thumbtack
pencil with an eraser or craft stick

Directions:

1. Cut two squares of the same size from construction paper.

2. Fold the corner of each square over into a triangle.

3. Fold each triangle in half. Unfold the paper.

4. Using crayons or markers, decorate one side of each square with the Juneteenth flag.

5. Put the undecorated sides of each square together. Cut along each of the four fold lines, about halfway to the middle of the square.

6. Still holding both squares together, punch four holes—one in each corner on one side of your cuts.

Pinwheels

7. Gently gather the point you hole-punched from each corner to the center. Be careful not to crease the paper.

8. Push a push-pin or thumbtack through the center to attach the pinwheel to the side of a pencil's eraser or into a craft stick.

9. Blow gently on your Juneteenth pinwheel to watch it spin!

*Safety Note: Be sure to ask for help from an adult, if needed, to complete this project.

Glossary

abolitionists Individuals who believed that slavery was wrong and helped to end it.

ancestor A person from whom one is descended.

civil rights Basic human rights, like voting and going to school, that are guaranteed by law to all people.

Civil War The war fought in the United States between the North and South from 1861 to 1865. One of the main causes was slavery.

emancipation Freedom from slavery.

Emancipation Proclamation President Abraham Lincoln's order on January 1, 1863, to free all slaves in the United States.

General Order Number 3 An announcement read aloud in Galveston, Texas, on June 19, 1865, that told slaves that they were free.

indentured servants People who agree to work for a certain period of time to pay off a debt, such as the cost of coming to another country.

secede When part of a country separates from the rest of the country.

tradition The practice of passing down customs, beliefs, or other knowledge from parents to children.

Learn More

Books

Johnson, Angela. *All Different Now: Juneteenth, the First Day of Freedom.* New York, NY: Simon & Schuster Books for Young Readers, 2014.

Jordan, Denise. *Juneteenth.* Portsmouth, NH: Heinemann, 2008.

Levy, Janey. *Juneteenth: Celebrating the End of Slavery.* New York, NY: Rosen, 2003.

Olson, Kay Melchisedech. *Africans in America, 1619–1865.* Mankato, MN: Blue Earth Books, 2003.

Peppas, Lynn. *Juneteenth.* New York, NY: Crabtree Publishing, 2010.

Websites

History of Juneteenth
www.juneteenth.com
Find out more about the history of Juneteenth.

Social Studies for Kids: The Importance of Juneteenth
www.socialstudiesforkids.com/articles/holidays/juneteenth.htm
Some background and facts about Juneteenth.

Index

A

abolitionists, 24
amendments, 12–14
ancestors, 7

B

barbeque, 5, 17, 25

C

civil rights, 24
Civil War, 10–12
Confederate states, 10
Constitution, 12–14

D

Douglass, Frederick, 24

E

Edwards, Al, 20
Emancipation
    Proclamation, 11, 12,
    17, 23

F

Fourth of July, 5, 10
freedom, 5, 7, 11–12, 26

G

General Order Number 3,
    12, 15, 17, 23
Granger, Gordon, 12, 15

I

indentured servants, 8
Independence Day, 10

J

Juneteenth
    becomes a holiday,
        20–22
    celebrating, 5, 7, 14,
        15–19, 22, 23–26

K

King, Dr. Martin Luther,
    Jr., 24

L

Lincoln, Abraham, 11

P

parades, 5, 15, 23
Parks, Rosa, 24
plantations, 8, 10

R

Revolutionary War, 10
rodeos, 19, 25

S

school, 7, 24
slavery, 5, 6–7, 8–14, 15,
    17, 24, 26

T

Texas, 7, 12, 14, 15, 19, 20,
    22
Thirteenth Amendment,
    14
Tubman, Harriet, 24

U

Union, 10, 12

V

Virginia, 8

W

Washington Juneteenth,
    25–26